Joan,

Gyda photo dymunia'd da.

Roy.

A small token for a large debt.

THE
THIRD
DAY

THE THIRD DAY

LANDSCAPE & THE WORD

An Anthology of Poems and Photographs

Edited by KATHY MILES

Photography by JOHN REED

With a preface by CLAY JONES

First Impression—May 1995

ISBN 1 85902 154 9

This book is published with the support of
the Arts Council of Wales.

Printed in Wales by
J. D. Lewis and Sons Ltd.,
Gomer Press, Llandysul, Dyfed

This book is dedicated to the work of the Welsh Historic Gardens Trust, who provided the inspiration for the original idea, and whose support has been invaluable during its compilation.

Contents

Contents (continued)

Acknowledgements

Acknowledgements are due to the following, for their help and advice during the compilation of this anthology:

The Welsh Historic Gardens Trust, CADW, the National Trust, Dyfed Wildlife Trust, *New Welsh Review*, *P.N Review*, *Outposts*, *Poetry Wales*, *Planet*, John Carr, David Austin, University of Wales Lampeter, Peter Miles, Jennie Bracher, Sian Spink, the National Monuments Record, Aberystwyth, R.R. Rockingham Gill, C.W. Marx and William Powell Wilkins.

With special thanks to Elisabeth Whittle (CADW) and Michael Norman (Welsh Historic Gardens Trust) for their invaluable help with the indexing.

Some of these poems have previously appeared in the following magazines:
Illumination: *New Welsh Review*
Meurig Dafydd to his Mistress: *P.N Review*
Portmeirion: *Anglo-Welsh Review*. This poem also appears in
Perspective Lessons, *Virtual Lines* (Rockingham Press).

Preface

The New World Thesaurus defines the noun 'landscape' as 'natural scenery, scene, scenery, or panorama'. The verb it defines as 'do the landscaping....., put in the lawn and shrubbery'. In tune with both definitions our Welsh countryside is an amalgam of the natural and the contrived and is arguably none the worse for that.

The once lovely valleys of South Wales fell prey to the industrial revolution, which tore at the landscape and created monstrous mountains of waste. Today the coal and the ore are gone, the land has been 'scaped' by both Man and Nature and those valleys are green again.

In North Wales, the slate quarries took their toll of natural beauty but in Mid Wales the land largely escaped the cut and thrust of industry. Amid the pastoral peace of Powys lies Powis Castle and its famed hanging garden terraces. Flanked by the great manicured yews, the richly planted chalk-soil terraces sweep down to the floor of the Formal Garden and its equally formal borders stocked with colourful herbaceous perennials and roses. Beyond the Great Lawn is the Woodland Garden where the soil changes dramatically from alkaline to acid and rhododendrons grow lush and lovely in company with hydrangeas and magnolias.

We who are Welsh by birth and tongue are justly proud of our Principality. Its landscape and its lilting language have inspired writers of both poetry and prose over the ages. As the twentieth century fades into history we give thanks for the beauty and the bounty that are our birthright amid the meadows and mountains of our homeland.

D. B. Clay Jones

Through the Yew Tunnel

The Third Day was conceived out of an amalgamation of two ideas: the growing national recognition of the richness of the built heritage of Wales, and in recent years, the restoration, or rising up, of many neglected sites, characterised by the nature of the work done at places such as Erddig and Powis. This restoration - the light at the end of the tunnel - is central to many of the poems. In particular, we wanted to emphasise not only the 'lost' heritage of Wales, but also to include sites currently part of ongoing restoration projects. To this end, poets were guided by a site-list prepared by the Welsh Historic Gardens Trust. While not prescriptive, it was intended to direct the writing towards those places felt to be of special architectural or historical importance. The anthology therefore deliberately portrays a landscape of both the familiar and the unknown. Though guided by the list, poets selected their own sites, and many have close personal or even family associations with them; in addition to the more famous places lies an intimate, inner landscape that the reader may be unfamiliar with. Partly for this reason, it was important that an index should be included which would identify the sites in both geographical and historical terms. The reader in this way is led through a verbal and visual landscape, founded in a Wales to be discovered on the map as well as in the mind.

Wales has a diverse historic landscape which has traditionally been a focal point for artists and writers. The landscape of a country, of course, enters its culture in its 'sense of place' shaped by socio-economic, political and historical factors, coalescing into individual experience. Landscape is not simply where you are. It is also who you are. A place cannot be seen apart from its context. It is living, shape-shifting in response to the needs of the individual, industry, and urban development. To write about landscape therefore becomes an act of re-creation, an acknowledgement of the poet's own place in the cultural development of the country.

All of the contributors to the anthology are either Welsh, or have lived, or still live, in Wales. Their work represents a very personal view; they are inhabitors of the landscape rather than passing visitors. There is a sense of dispossession and disinheritance which comes through strongly as a uniting overall theme. This sense of loss is demonstrated not only by those 'exiled' poets now living outside Wales, but also by those who write from within their own country, but are perhaps disinherited both from their own landscape and the 'lost' sites on which many of the poems focus. This is summarised in 'Plas yn Rhiw' by R.S. Thomas, which is a poem of lost voices, 'sea voices lingering in a shell', in which the loss expressed is an ache that, at the end, can never be assuaged.

The emotional tone of the poems ranges from gentleness to anger, from quiet reflectivity to intellectual persuasion. In some landscapes the reader is made to feel easy and familiar, both with the site and by the descriptive nature of the poem. In others, the landscape holds a defined or implied threat, an uneasiness in which the surroundings are not always comfortable or secure. As the poems vary in tone, so they also embody a range of different landscapes, covering many hundreds of years of Welsh history, from the Neolithic to the present, and encompassing both the private and the civic, the untamed and the formal. Some poems portray strongly visual and individual experiences, while others are narrative in style, and on occasions the poet has adopted a particular persona in order to explore aspects of the site more freely. The physical and literal standpoints also differ. Some poets withdraw from the site in order to place it in its surrounding landscape. Others take the reader inside the house or site, so that we experience an intimacy not only with the place, but also with the inhabitants. At other times the poet maintains a strictly controlled poetic and personal distance that allows the reader a simultaneous interior and exterior view of the landscape. The uniting factors are the voices and the sense of place, drawing on both individual experience and the political and historical landscape.

Photographic decisions were taken as part of an integrated approach to the editorial process. It was important that neither word nor image should be allowed to dominate; the aim is that they should enhance and complement each other. In some cases, poets specified their photographic requirements. Otherwise the professional judgement of the photographer was used. Sometimes a clear representational shot was called for, or the site deliberately distanced in order to allow the surrounding landscape to prevail. At other times a much more physical interaction took place, so that we actually entered the landscape - including lakes and waterfalls - in order to obtain the best representation of the central image of the poem. This means that in some cases the reader has to 'work' harder at interpreting the poem, and on other occasions, the photograph. It also became apparent that we did not always discover what the poet had seen. The landscape was both an intervening and shaping presence. Visits to the same place on separate occasions produced different experiences. This altered our perception both as passive onlookers and interactive participants. What is represented, therefore, is not necessarily the exact landscape that the poet saw, nor will the reader find what we discovered. What is presented is a particular moment in time. While we inevitably changed the landscape by our presence, so must every visitor who passes through it.

Of the sites depicted in the anthology, three - Beaupre, Hafod and Castell Coch - are represented by more than one poem, emphasising their symbolic importance as significant phases in the built heritage of Wales. The architectural history has already been well documented. Wales is, of course, renowned for its castles, both for the early *cestyll* of the Welsh princes, and the later Norman fortifications which still dominate the landscape. Many of these castles were later abandoned or, like Beaupre - originally a medieval site - rebuilt through the centuries as the need for greater comfort combined with a desire to incorporate innovative architectural styles. Beaupre, like many of these modified sites, was successively occupied through the centuries. Many of the houses of the *uchelwyr* were - for economic, social and physical reasons - smaller than their English counterparts, and styles were affected by the geological characteristics of the region. 'Clustering' of sites is inevitable, occurring where the timber or stone available was particularly suitable for building. Welsh houses passed through the same range of architectural styles - and many of the same architects - as did English houses. Beaupre characteristically shows the effect of the widespread rebuilding programme that occurred in the sixteenth century, when the dissolution of the monasteries and the breakdown of the Marcher lordships led to the acquisition of rich land by new owners, and the subsequent desire to redesign and refurbish older properties and gardens in the prevailing styles of the era. Rebuilt in the sixteenth century as an Elizabethan mansion, Beaupre typically incorporates a mixture of Tudor gothic and renaissance, retaining many of its medieval aspects with the addition of new features.

The eighteenth century saw the construction of some of the finest houses in Wales. Styles ranged from the simple elegance of Georgian and Regency, to the introduction of pseudo-medieval gothic. From this period come some masterpieces of design, including the sham castles of Clytha, Gnoll, Wynnstay, Garth and many others. The increasing trend towards Romanticism, and the greater attention being paid to garden and landscape design culminated in the Picturesque movement at the end of the century, stunningly defined at Hafod and Piercefield, where the divide between nature and artifice was blurred, and formality abandoned in favour of the 'awful sublimity' of the untamed landscape.

Castell Coch is again a representative site, in this case of the wealth created by the development of the coal and steel industries of South Wales in the late nineteenth century. While buildings for industry were generally simple and utilitarian, accompanied by a new supporting system of communications, increasing wealth gave rise to a number of impressive but eccentric indulgences of architectural neo-gothic fantasy, which included Castell Coch, Gwrych and Cardiff Castle in particular. From this period onwards we also see the development of civic architecture, parks, and the founding of many new communities in Wales.

Much of this heritage has, over the years, been lost to the natural landscape. Factors involved include neglect and lack of interest in the sites, compounded by the very real damage done during the times of the Civil War and the dissolution of the monasteries, which had earlier taken their toll of many finely designed buildings. More recently, the death duties introduced in 1894 led many owners to demolish parts of their property in order to avoid the high payments. Requisitioning of older buildings during the Second World War left many of them abandoned.

Although the first Ancient Monuments Protection Act appeared on the statute books in 1882, it is only in comparatively recent times that conservation has begun in earnest. In 1984 CADW was set up. Its remit includes houses, ancient monuments, castles, bridges and much vernacular architecture. In addition to the work of the National Trust, more and more County Councils are also taking restoration work on board, and private trusts and bodies are being set up, with the aim of recovering and restoring what is left. The Welsh Historic Gardens Trust has taken on Hafod as a special project, but many more sites have now been listed, and much hard work done, in the forefront of which is the requirement for much greater public awareness of the need to conserve.

Compiling and working on the anthology has, throughout, been a learning experience. Walking through the ancient yew tunnel at Aberglasney we passed in a sense under the landscape. At the other end, light, and the shock of the large ruined house. That sudden recognition is part of the landscape experience. As Gillian Clarke says in 'Hafod', 'the idea of a house is stronger than walls'. So is the idea of the landscape much more than fields or hills or valleys. It is the formal organisation of memory and desire, a 'sense of place' that encompasses social, historical and cultural perceptions. In caring for, restoring, and writing about this landscape, we are not doing it for ourselves, nor just to honour the achievements of the past. Coming out of the tunnel, into that 'elusive brilliance', we open the future.

Kathy Miles

BERTHOLEY HOUSE

At Bertholey House

'lone white house, symbol of a world of wonder...'
Arthur Machen

The forest hangs in its uneasy heat.
Bracken bends and whispers, crisp with spore.
A beetle cracks its hot black carapace
increasing a glint of wing. Down long
green tracks you walked towards the house

where lizards flicker on the baking arch,
light tasting their deep crevices like tongues.
Broken open by the flames' red fingers
something has escaped. You stood among bees
speaking to me in a haze of thyme.

Candles once, and tasselled red brocade.
Bound books that crackled in the open case.
Your fingers in the charred grit.
A poet's dream, you said, a tower in a tale. When
nothing's left of all our words but light.

Catherine Fisher

BEAUPRE CASTLE

Beaupre Castle

How is it possible to forget so much?
We came chattering out of the lanes
St Hilary way. Beaupre, Bewper -
not a castle then, not a ruin. In the old
stone kitchen warmed by a summer fire
I sat and laughed with the rest, all of us young;
I was the stranger, welcomed and quizzed.
Three daughters of the farm poured tea.

The two great porches I know now
from books, but don't remember.
Then, there was arching dark
after the white lane, an ancientness
growing from the rough utilitarian garden,
grandeur comfortably mixed
with everyday, all just a stage-set
for a dance of happiness over shadows.

I should have liked to think of Richard Bassett
building his storeyed porch, and wonder
how much truth Iolo put into his legends.
I should have read the words in stone,
'Say couldst thou ever find
or ever hear or see
worldly wretch or coward prove
a faithful friend to be?'
                    But that
was for another time, not this
tunnel-visioned, unregretted afternoon,
when the parched lanes offered up
puffs of white dust, and grey dank walls
softened and held our taut excited laughter.

Ruth Bidgood

HAFOD (THE ROBBER'S CAVE)

Hafod

Frail architecture, its fine lines rased
from the tangled pleasure grounds below the ridge,
where the idea of a house is stronger
than walls, a fallen roof, temple and bridge.
Even the waterfall, Laporte's engraving
or the real thing after heavy rain, reflects
stonework and windows of a house
turned to a memory of the picturesque
young Turner painted; or Coleridge, passing this way
from Devil's Bridge over the mountain track,
astonished, perhaps, by a glimpse of Xanadu
one afternoon two hundred Augusts back.

Here Thomas Johnes' dream grew tall,
the wilderness flowering in his mind
while the carriage stumbled the stony road from Hereford.
The last twelve miles on foot through rain and wind,
driven by visions of a great estate
rising above the river under Pumlimon,
his mountains clothed in larch and oak and ash,
three million reddening in late November sun.
Jane's lists remain, her smugglers' silks,
four kinds of lace, muslin for an apron,
her twenty yards of ribbon for a bonnet.
'Brocaded silks,' she wrote, 'are all the tone.'

All gone, but the idea of quiet rooms,
the octagon library under its cupola
where he worked late on ancient manuscripts,
their words flickering under the candelabra.
The end of the line. The bright young naturalist,
Mariamne, beloved only child,
dead at twenty seven. His fortune spent, a house and a class
in ruins, the gardens turned back to the wild.
Below the mulch perhaps a gilded flake, a marbled skull,
a peacock's feather in the grass, shadows
that could be the disposition of a house,
each fall a myth of sun-reflecting windows.

Gillian Clarke

ABERGAVENNY CASTLE

The Abergavenny Murders

Climbing the castle mound,
above this prosperous little town, with its hanging baskets
in bloom on each shop-front, scented with alyssum and geraniums.
Looking at Usk and its water meadows, and the circle of
mountains.

They act plays in the keep.
Poison and stabbings are quite familiar. Here is a man
hiding in a chest in a lady's bedchamber.
He is just about to leap out and make mischief.

At Sarajevo
Gavrilo Princip's footsteps sunk in the pavement
in the exact spot where he stood to hurl his bomb.

Not here, though.
Giant copper beeches grow in the remnants
of the banqueting hall, and cast huge shadows.
Blood does not last eight hundred years, and continually
we tread over the grass where there were murders.

Merryn Williams

LLANMIHANGEL PLACE

Llanmihangel y Fro

Catherine Thomas remembers her ancestral home as she sets out to wed William James of Pencoed, Capel Llanilltern, in 1849

I have a rendezvous with love, at Pencoed y Capel,
toward the dawn, on higher ground.
I have the blessing of Betws, of those who gave me life,
and He is with me.

God gave me green pastures,
my two kittens, wheaten bread and junket,
opened my eyes to His fair creation.
For all this I am bounden, in awe and humility
as I trace my name my father carved in the dovecot wall.

Yet, bereft, heartstunned,
my mind lingers by the home that made us.
What know I of the wanton world?
Llanmihangel was cradle and nurse,
mighty fortress in troubled time.

Its every lichened stone I know;
red and blue lanterns in the corn;
holy scents of rosemary and new mown hay;
rabbits racing for the hedgerows;
heads bowed at harvest home;
firelight bright in the thronged kitchen;
cerddi swynol Iolo saer maen;
Sion Blaenhenwysg's fiddle yearning, *llofft y stabal.*
"When I was a child, I saw as a child... ."

How, *o lan Elai*, shall I see Llanmihangel?
How hear again its soaring larks?
How then shall I recall my Zion?
How unlock its gates?

Three keys I take, to heart's desiring:

From the stream, a pebble.

From the peacock, a feather.

From the garden, a root of thyme.

H.G.A. Hughes

From Small Beginnings......
Gwrych Castle

Saint Michael winces at Hesketh's window,
mourns quickset Hen Wrych, hearth to home-grown folk,
breathes absolution for fading folly.

       *   *   *

Gwrych grew brash yet graceful in green acres
tan yr ogof, rhwng ddwy afon,
well matched with gentle neighbours,
its bounty full for every simple need,
deep set for settled centuries.

       *   *   *

From Abbotsford, Tuscany and Tyrol
heady blast and sweet miasma wrought overweening dreams
that called for stone upon stone
and yet more stone, traceries in Mersey iron.

Margaret's sainted dedication,
Cinmael, Parys-proud and Hampton-dazed,
Bodelwyddan and Broadlane,
fever-spurred to outdo Babel's reach to heaven;
fanned the grand illusion, the vain assertion;
wall after wall, Hesketh tower on topsy turret,
swagger stables and marble stair,
pictured simulacrum of Jerusalem on sea,
fay landscape beyond Claude's conception.
Welsh Wales watched and wondered;
her masons blessed each vaulting whim
to loom large in eyes of God and man,
lamented their passing so long delayed.

       *   *   *

GWRYCH CASTLE

Lady Eleanor's sturdy tower still scans the shore
yet only Gwrych's sheep serve a purpose
and the wild immensity of the banquet hall
shrills and echoes to rats at play.
Ghosts wrench from the grand organ
Gwrych's *memento mori*, anthem for the wanton dead:
vanitas vanitatis, all is vanity,
Umberto Eco's 'real fake'.

H.G.A. Hughes

CWM

Cwm Merddog

It is called *limen inferum* the threshold
The boundary stone by which you know
The other side far from home
Beyond the playing street.

Stone whitened before eight marks the start
Of every journey and return to the school
Whose small-paned windows and beaded
Curtain exist only in memory.

Below the doorstone of my house unknown
Unperceived by all excepting me is
As was the custom an infant boy
Curled lovingly in death.

Carved in the lintel the *limen superum*
Three figures hooded and long-shadowed.

When I return it is to the blasphemy of a car-park
Where once the pit-head brought Marine Street to a
Full-stop, and a hole of its own digging into which
The Miners' Institute has disappeared.
This village lost half its name when it was built
Dog-legged across the Ebbw Fawr and the railway;
Its classical uniformity neutralising the natural
Fall of field and valley floor; over rooftops rose
The grey-green ramparts perched with pigeon-lofts
And improbable allotments.
At night from Currie Street the fiery mountains
Volcanoed white hot slag in the north where now
A waterfall, graceful, Japannois, bespangles a
Coal-black pool.

Of the three shadowed hooded ones, the Cucullati,
One holds a thread, one a measuring rod,
And one the terrible shears.

J. Roy Birch

PLAS YN RHIW

Plas yn Rhiw

This garden is reflected
in an under-water garden.
When summer arrives
the wrack has the smell
of the bitterest of flowers
but domesticated by sunlight.

The tones of the old ladies
are sea voices lingering
in a shell. Roses hang
their heads as their presences
pass by; but pansies lift theirs
with velvet in their expression.

Between Irish yews
the air is a window
upon a Welsh sea
often dishevelled, although
not to-day, where distant
mountains vie with it in blueness.

The house, though old, reposes
on an earlier foundation,
sunning itself on the hill's side.
The wind in the rafters
at night is as an echo
of the conversation of princes.

It has been reclaimed,
delivered out of the clutches
of dandelion and ivy,
taken in care. Yet there is an ache
here the many contributions
of visitors can never assuage.

R.S. Thomas

BODFUAN

Bodfuan, Lleyn

There are words for you in another language
Hall of low meadows
Larch-fringed marsh
There are words for the snipe and black-headed gull
Hall below crag
And sunken hill forest
There are words which pass through prisms of
                              your windows
Without refracting
There are words you remember
Without knowing why
In all the flares of rhododendron
And swallows swooping on shallows of scree
Your walls are held in a stone language
Sea breezes coming freely
Translating where they will.

David Annwn

LADY'S BEDROOM, CASTELL COCH

Lady's Bedroom, Castell Coch

picture her nightdress-clad
preparing for that wide-slung bed
she adjusts pillows opens sheets
waits for the shuddering door's
gape but observe crystal globes

level with head heart foot
reflecting every candle
to light her bed with enclosed flames
she is an incandescent moon
plucked from Glamorgan darkness

which gathers in soft clouds
now she stares into one glass globe
its planet spins before blurred eyes
continents seas separate
with every tossed candle flame

slow breath of life circles
inside six thinly blown spheres
parallelled by sighing as she
hovers above unending curves
phrasing her song of wonder

but rasping door hinges
snap the cord of her trance plummet
her into that closed married world
where candles are extinguished
and star worlds melt in darkness

Alison Bielski

ABERGLASNEY

Aberglasney Enigma

Peacefully, in crisp and winter sunlight,
December fifteen, seventeen fifty seven,
The Cambrian poet, painter, priest John Dyer
Died in a damp house in the fens of Lincoln.

He said 'I die easy', unearthing his
Single talent, a few poems dropped when he
Was easy and young, playing in sunshine
At Aberglasney, under God's eye in Wales.

Aberglasney: the house now splits, cracks, rots
Like beechmast; goats alone inhabit rooms
Paved with plaster; limp leaves on terraces
Sodden after summer mourn the mysterious
Garden whose loping porticos and raised
Walks import an alien Italian strut
To the Towy's banks, as it lurches, rolls
And shoulders its way to the western sea.

Who planned, who built this cryptoportical
Elegant extravaganza garden,
Out of its time, misplaced, magnificent?
Or does it merely echo vanished rhythms
From a monastic past? Scholars debate.
Green thoughts in shades, ideas in airy walks
Lie buried here in wet brickdust and rubble,
Overlaid all with beechleaves, brambles, bracken.

You must come here in Winter, if you seek
Truth. Historians prefer walls bare, trees
Leafless, faded flowerbeds frozen, soil turned
Sour, and all tones dun. They fur their gloves with
Facts against cold, bright fantasies. Go, measure
The angles and returns. Go, analyse
Your brickwork, interrogate each arcade.
This lost garden still survives your questions.

You must come in April, if you can bear
Spring's uncertainty, the daffodil's trespass.
But never look for simple resurrections
In this garden. In garden arts there is
No going back; and entropy remains
A one-way street. Do not strip this green place
Bare of its mysteries. Leave some. Let it
Like us, like all of us, die easy, silent.

Brian R. Morris

Tan-yr-Allt

He came here with an idea
of light, space and improvement.
It was in the air of Fron Yw
on a shelf over the Clwyd valley
and in the verandah'd improvement
of Dolmelynllyn.

Madocks had a way of seeing quickly
what should be done, and pushing through.
With John Williams, an idea,
a few sketches, Tremadog -
Town Hall, square, hotel, homes,
even a woollen factory - sprang together.

Penrhyn Quarry slates of superior quality
made his house's long roof.
Here Shelley drew his pen over Queen Mab
and had his life threatened by an outraged neighbour.
From here, like Noah, he could oversee his work.
His new house, Morfa Lodge, also on a high ledge
was being made and landscaped,
overlooking the Cob and the Port,
for his final, married return.

But Paris claimed him, not the Glaslyn.

The glassy lake that was is no more,
but the Glaslyn is still untamed,
the sea filtering the reeds;
Madocks's embankment carries the hooting trains,
miniature, brassed and busy
with a purpose the artery
through which trade and now tourism flowed.

TAN-YR-ALLT

Tan-yr-Allt, its casement, not sash windows,
its verandah'd and flowing roof -
a house turned around in Regency style
from the farmhouse it was - looks out
with a certain grandeur,
testament to the vision of a singular man.

John Idris Jones

MARGAM

Margam

In the West Wing, decorum
kept a chamber, venerable
linenfold panels a schoolroom
in wooden skirts. Stiff
children were never taught there,
nor cried their misery
to the walls.

An airless, unexpected hush
fell on paying visitors, comments
deadened by wood, stilled
by the unrocked cot, pristine
hobbyhorse, unbanged drum.

An English primer, full
of untried phrases, unnecessary
words, lay open, astonished,
mouth gaping dumb
eloquence.

Perhaps a lord, heirless,
and his taciturn wife, passed
like paying visitors through
the joyless room, his eyes glazed,
her eyes averted, stiff skirts
decorous.

From an East Wing window
maybe she could look across the park
at the ruined abbey
where decorum keeps a chamber, tiny,
with linenfold panels
of stone, the airless hush
undisturbed by cries of children.

Neal Mason

PORTMEIRION

Portmeirion, An Advert

Not merely Style but an architecture of the mind

and plunging down an uncertain path, pursued by rain,
not Fantasy but a way of reading symbols all too real.
A dog's head. A dog's head: no, good God -
a moss covered stump. But the book said -
I know, it's around here somewhere, by some
Pythagorean angle. Meanwhile we have at Easter
the highest summer yet; nothing has led us to expect
that bright rhodo-red, tall as a folk tale
against the dripping stone. Stumbling through bamboo
we guess at the coast. Come to it, past
tabletops of wood we think might be rock
but are not. Then the Celtic requiem of bitter greens,
an ancient sea-edged frieze of sheep-bitten
unhistory. And this shore this gregarious
global village. And both as real.

Turning back to the silly village
is returning to what poetry always toys with:
human life as Allegory, ideas
as concretely embodied, if lightly built,
marvellous struggles with space and time;
all pure insanity unless God exists -
and may go at times yellow-stockinged;
or it is how life should be and
how we mould our landscapes, how
Beauty is a manmade concept. Every Home
is here, if not every house. The hotel's
burnt down though; time trembles in thistledown,
Poetry goes to seed or runs to prose, but inside
one more distant gazebo, the whole prospect's held
in a private film, a dream of buildings
playing in the dark of God's numb skull.
Then there are the inhabitants.

You are not more real than they:
Wayland the Smith, Hans the Host,
Raffael the Bellringer,
Demeter the Summer-bringer,
Buddha, the serene, meditating flimsy stone,
predicting the eternity of the mayfly,
Flora, queen of Carnival,
Wren, judger of the Interval,
Hercules cleaning a moulded ceiling
(Comedy and Tragedy whispering in the wings
of a magpie crossing the aged Globe
a straining Atlas manages to hold
from toppling into the waiting Ocean),

Neptune who rains in the hall,
Punning Pan and Thalia,
someone Biblical, blessing us all.
And these milling extras in period clothes....

Look around now at the inner townscape.
See the Gods and Goddesses survive the fickle times,
'Renaissance' to Deco to Festival lines:
return to the worst fate of all - to be human.
Leave by the drab back of the facade -
the half onion dome, the plain Conveniences,
the ignominious track. You could have stayed,
to talk to Admiral Benbow-Williams-is-it/was it?,
sail off in that boat of solid concrete,
kiss amid the scalloped graffiti, add your own.

Now return home to find the windows
painted on the wall and a puzzling view

that's never been seen before. And something missing:
like a forgotten line, or key
that childhood lost in some garden
in a summer

left

far

behind

Chris Bendon

POWIS CASTLE

Powis Castle

Moated in the deer park,
Italian terraces still hang here,
drip above a more fashionable
wilderness. Only ferns, ivy

now swirl the cool eddies
of an Orangery washed
by fuchsia, purple-monkshood,
a spray of tea-scented rose.

Baroque pleasure pools have gone,
but urns jut as breakwaters
into this raised tide of flowers.
Box and yew billow paths, tumble

down to rill the formal garden
where avenues of apple and vine
buoy towards a dry fountain,
float in gilded marjoram.

Julie Rainsbury

LLANERCHAERON

Llanerchaeron: A Private View

The caretaker is kind, unbolts the faded door:
"But don't enter the buildings - and don't stay long."
Pass through the wall, and into a Narnian climate -
The climate of privilege; as if the stone boundaries
Had raised an old marquee of milder sky.
Horizontals hold the power here; wide-shouldered
Espaliers rail the walks, lilliputian hedges
Quarter the borders; the centre is hushed expanse,
Levels of turf and water; whole kitchen gardens
Lie back by the walls in beds raised ankle-high.
Even the delicate ribs of the hothouse roofs
Yield to the charm; they are sinking into their brambles
Like so many Sleeping Beauties. You speak in whispers
Not to break the spell. Time has unlocked
The barrier of privilege, but time will also bring
Changes, invasions. There is no staying long.

Stevie Krayer

CASTELL COCH

Kidwelly

The accent of place
in a complex land
where the Gwendraeth rivers
unite like twins
to meet the Tywi.
The sleeping castle at peace
like Turner's painting,
the changeable sky and the rich fields
all witnesses through time
to crossings and survivals,
the inward brightness of landscape
a substance of light passing through.

Castell Coch

It could have been
uprooted from the high banks
of a Rhinescape valley,
the conical turrets of this red castle
at home in a Victorian
pre-Disneyland,
where later
Alan Ladd pretended in chains
to be its only recorded prisoner.
There are of course
more substantial castles in Wales,
reliably ancient,
a pedigree,
without the intervention or riches
of a Burges or a Bute,
but phoenix jokes of sandstone
in a Welsh fairyland
could be what sham
history is all about.

B. W. Beynon

GARDEN FESTIVAL, EBBW VALE

Garden Festival, 1992

Hey! you girl, bending in vale of Ebbw,
fingering soft bloodshot silk of poppies,
you think they frill for your pleasure, though new
tendrils would climb on you if they could, would

grow on you scarlet as your lips will, curl
round your head as your hair will, if they could.
Stood bonny in soil dark with death of coal,
running with rust from bright steel, they nod bells,

but never for you, for the fly coyly,
for fine-furred rapacious legs of the bee -
they draw nothing from the innocent touch
of girls, for Madame has decreed blindly

that on an Earth empty of humankind,
her poppies shall continue to unfurl,
swell, curl, make curtsey to her breeze, and mate
always, needing neither girls nor gardens.

Edmund Davies

GELLI AUR (FROM THE FISHPOND)

From The Terrace: Gelli Aur

The older years hang here, like yellowing leaves.
By the late built house, hard-chiselled shape, we stand
In the splintered rain by where the parapet divides
And frames the valley filled with ageing trees.

Our thoughts are older than the woodlands,
Far back beyond this stranded place which speaks
Impermanence in stone; Scottish cairngorm
Set on, not in, its intertwining trees. Cold grove

Gold grove; the names are right these chill October
Afternoons. Behind us is the gold, beyond the steel
Sharp edges of the house, where groves in tiered trees
Soar, curvet, mould their patterns, black and green

And gold. (But cold, coldly stir the dark firs below.)
And now below, and down beyond us, where the Towy's
Doused by the iron rain and the rusty streaking leaves,
Voices call from the valley (only the sound of leaves,

Of the restless damp trees) names older than
This terrace and these trees. Across the valley Merlin
Lies (or Spenser lied) somewhere in the woods of Dinevor,
Across the valley lies Grongar Hill, that harmless

Quiet poem-hill, and here below this house, down
Where we might try to trace the old house,
(If we had time, if it had time,) its dull damp shade,
Where Taylor amidst these rustling hills, lived and

Thought, scratched out, rethought, re-made again
Those words, not of this alien house, but from
Those native secret hills within his mind.
Hills look to misty hills. Rain closes down;

Merlin will sleep within his cave unstirred
This narrowing afternoon. Grongar Hill, unvisited,
Will dream beneath the purposeful grey clouds,
And on the page, will be another tattered leaf

At Gelli Aur.

David Palmer

Castell Henllys

The world today has a blue voice;
a late bee thrums in its ear.
Nubians snuffle the slow light,
squirrel their way through sycamore.
Here there's a herb-garden,
chive, poppy, apple-mint. Stealing
foxgloves. A blackbird screams my theft.

On the top, roundhouses, carefully
made from wicker. New as the long
tea-room dug into post holes below.
Dried skins, stone hearths, a scatter
of ash at the centre. Cold fire,
waiting for the iron touch of a pot.

We fiercely defend our privacy,
slope off, quick-footed, to diggings
cut square-on in the hillside.
From here, sight is unmarred.
We chalk our names on slate;
graffiti, etching soft stone easily.

The sun dips suddenly. Casts molten
bars on the bark, an ambush
flush with the branches. We forge
our own weapons. Broken off,
a chunk of marble thrown palm
to palm hones to a glow of blood.
A small pig rushes us, squealing.

Now we're forgetting the names of things.
Leaves are burnt umber, but
we can't remember their genus.
The path's slippery. Old shoes,
tread gone, tumble us downwards.
It is a path for bare feet,
for getting a grip with the toes.

CASTELL HENLLYS

As the sky begins to bleach,
lyre-song of gathered birds
edges us out along the river bank.
Grey ghosts lift up their devil-heads
to watch us sift the leaves.
Stepping back into the blue voice, a chaos
of shadows, voices, shuffling goats.

Kathy Miles

LLANTARNAM ABBEY

Llantarnam Abbey Gardener

Nicholas Harold Hob, all fiery
with gold and silver smiles,
whistles along the terrace
cheerfully yearning for acid rain,
for corrosive clutch of ivy,

but then scans in vain
over musketeer and archer
for rust that creeps the stone,
sulphur that bleeds
from the wall's quickened mortar.

Anxious, he bends under the arches.
Ah! there, a tiny seed, shy
where a Master Mason's trowel slipped,
dropped by the savage robin for future
pollination by witless breezes,

a Christmas berry, plump with poison
to make the lungs of children
balloon before they fall.
All is well for his Mistress -
this is how her garden grows.

Edmund Davies

ST. TWROG'S STONE

St Twrog's Stone

'Undeniably an erratic. This location
is inexplicable.' Rubbing it with a finger,
the geologist confesses puzzlement. 'Where the hell
is the rest of the moraine?'

Twrog, the son of Ithel Hael,
sailed from Britanny to escape the migrant Franks.
Pagans - lank and greasy hair, tattoos,
a thin language. Inclined to savage practices,
an alien cuisine. He fetched up
in this riverine sanctuary where the Dwyryd squirms
adderlike to the open sea, and oak trees
command the tossed salad of the hillside.

But pagans crop up anywhere, like hunger
and pestilence. They lounge around, raise altars
to disreputable gods, cook fungi
that corrupt the metaphysics of the brain.

Who will blame Twrog, yanked from sleep
night after maddening night, plagued by owls,
distempered by the moon's strabismic eye?

Faith lent the saint the marble biceps
of a giant. He plucked the stone
from some granitic outcrop, bowled it down the slope
and scored himself a strike against their shrine.

I pause in the sunlight after a chilli
at The Grapes. It was one of Brian's blasters.
The church, with its chinese steeple,
black-hearted yews. The zoomorphic river.
And here, on the dumb stone,
impressions of thumb and finger.

No Christian these days can move as much
with bare hands. And I'm no Christian.

High in an oak the squirrels leap,
pouching sweet acorns. Empty cups
ricochet off the blue roof of my car.

Richard Poole

White Park Cattle

**The status of the Lord of Dinefwr is also adorned
with white cows, each with its head to the tail of
the next, with a bull between every twenty of them,
so as to fill the space from Argoel to the court
of Dinefwr.**

from: Hywel Dda, The Law

Gwenno Pinken Silken Shonken
Notty Betty Gently Lovely

A voice sounds through the scratches of the pen
Across two hundred years of tidy parkland
Calling these cattle home; a white herd walking.
One thousand years could change the names
And leave unfaltering their steady pace;
The rhythms of the year; the slippery calving,
The anxious bawling in the night,
The heart-deep grunting sigh at slaughter.

Lion Captain Trueman Baker
Ranter Royal Farmer Carver

White oxen built Dinefwr: dragged stone on wood
Up the east hill towards a setting sun.
The ox precedes the ploughman in the fields
Cutting the earth into a shape we recognise.
A shining calfskin makes the written page
Of law, of poetry, of peace and argument.
A churn sounds like a heartbeat through the stones
At Dinefwr, at Newton, through the park.

Peggy Posy Lilly Nelly
Fanny Kitty Cherry Beauty

The Lord Rhys rode this land, stopped
in the dark to hear the cattle breathe,
saw patches of white in the untidy woods.

71

DINEFWR

Star Bright Brisk Quick

A broken castle and an empty house:
This place keeps something stronger than the past:
A white cow in a white field, breath made visible
Raises a raven with her sudden call
Quickens the still woods at Dinefwr.

Helen Palmer

PENTRE IFAN BURIAL CHAMBER

Remains To Be Seen

It is the same land,
though the new witches call it Mother Earth
and an artist rebuilt it with angles and light.
I used to believe all the world had rock beneath it;
that you always bled after falling down.
On top of the blowing hill where even in summer
the breezes speak in winter whispers
I am small again:
pushing a chill breakfast towards
a multi-coloured sulk of chickens,
whilst behind me the scouring calves eject theirs.

A year since Mam died
and the yard still feels too big.
A year on and Mam is bigger still:
she has burst from the farm
and now the tractor trodden earth
ruts deep enough to sail boats on,
forms the line of her thighs.
Her stomach is the whole of the bottom field
she has a lime-pit belly button, the old one filled
with 'stupid dead cows and no-good dogs'.
I look up to her breasts; climbed, eaten and birthed on
by the dirty chewing sheep.
The cloud on Carningli hides her face
and I know she is naked, is cold,
for he has dressed the peggity man
in all her good clothes.

Sunday mornings - flowers for a vacant lot.
In the afternoons, the walk to Pentre Ifan
with a week's woe and a bunch of dying wildness
for my listening Mam under the big flat stone.
My sutures of distance rupture on return
to this Sunday place where souls were made of stone,

and Mam, when she had rotted to a pebble
would grow every time the rain
washed the silt and shit down from the fields.
So strong that feeling
I would not now be surprised
to pull from the cavity
a stone baby with earth for eyes.

Abi Hughes-Edwards

Adelina

She is creating history
where a castled garden blooms,
enticing warmth and harmony
to this ice-age valley of Wales.

From Craig-y-Nos, the Rock of Night,
to Cribarth top, the white Bear's Comb,
strange notes bewitch
the roaming sheep,
close by her walls,
her favoured home.

Verdi, Weber, erase old blood,
the thud of a caveman's spear,
the falling breath of a fallow deer.
Music unheard by Viking bands,
marauding legions come from Gaul.
Spanish cavalry, her kinsmen,
recalled to Rome
as an Empire falls.

Adelina nightingale, whose melody floats
through chandeliered, silk-walled halls,
winning the heart of a Prince of Wales,
his doting courtesans,
the muted applause of crested fans.

Through open doors her song descends
the terraced lawns to sweep the lake,
where ice-sheen crinolines of silvered gold,
reflect the water's reeded gleam.

Royalty walks; her stately trees
as guards of honour, marking this,
her territory,
her private principality.

CRAIG-Y-NOS CASTLE

Dark night now, dimmed castle lights,
but the mint she grew perfumes the park;
her voice lilting still through the leaves,

and the moist eavesdropping breeze.

Carole Morgan Hopkin

GREGYNOG

This Hand: Gregynog

This hand arrests you
at the crossroads

This hand is larger
than your own

It has never known
a wrist, a body

This hand stands upright
on the grass

It is unshaken
by any weather

Its cracks retain
the stain of time

This hand reflects
no mirror image

It is a left hand
sinister

This hand is stone-faced
open-handed

This hand gives nothing
This hand asks nothing

It holds no promise
of curse or blessing

Turn back, or walk
into the woods

This hand will offer
no direction

Joseph P. Clancy

ST. TRILLO'S CHAPEL

St. Trillo's Chapel Garden, Rhos-on-Sea

**The wall...impressed me from my first sight of it and so did
St. Trillo's chapel with its well of fresh water springing so near the salt
margin.**

David Jones, *Epoch and Artist*

Here, saint, in the sound of the waves,
Here the narrow border; paper-strewn roses,
Here at land's end for leper and traveller,
Here as a coach-stop for veteran and
Familiar war enemies healing their scars.
Here in the overturned boat-like buttress
Launched for the spirit; bulwarked
Against the driven flail of space.
This lost corridor of the forgotten saint,
This secret flower of freshwater
Stemming through the shade-flagged floor
Set by the salt-carnationed deep.
Here packed walls crouch down against it,
Outlast the neap and ebb of time,
Barely seeming to cling to the land
Of the living. You built so well:
Limpet on rock of the ages we call Dark.
Here, saint, with less than a spark
Of fluttering rushlight: your work hung on,
Left your prayer of stone right on the edge.

David Annwn

LLANDAFF COURT

Llandaff Court: Snow

Snow sifts down on the roof's grey forest;
caps the dead chimneys, dusts the pointed towers.
It is drifting high on the window-ledges,
but no sash is raised; no broom knocks

at the silence. Its soft weight snaps
the late roses; fills an old chain
of dry fishponds, slowly, like a dock
silting. Ships and coal built a house;

then the tide ebbed, and the hearths went dark,
and the sky empties so methodically.
The crevices of a stone lion's mane
whiten; smooth over, and he never stirs.

Sheenagh Pugh

STOUTHALL

Catherine at Stouthall

It must be the yellowest house in Wales!
What would John Lucas, who made it grow
in Palladian dignity from the old
farmhouse of his kin, think of this
mustard ostentation? No sure answer; he had
his quirks and whims. Yet this insistent colour
would not suit Catherine, daughter of shadow,
his dark-haired wife with melancholy eyes.

Could her Gower neighbours have met the bride
without a whisper in the mind, 'Glanareth'?
without a sickened scenting of her father's
spilt blood in that old house in hills to the north?
(And what had the delectable mother known? -
gone with her lover, and dragging two daughters
on her dubious journeying?) Perhaps
this dark girl kept a distance, let the quiet
of her coastland home, the structure of affection
and obligation, measured progress through
a given life, work on her mind. Or perhaps
that other mansion and its mayhem seemed
a half-heard story, not her own at all,
and neighbours' speculations were hardly noticed,
powerless to break the calm.

                    Her pictured face
is unreadable. It is hard to hold
the thought of her together with today's
exuberance of colour. She is more akin
to black water, deep grass, the dark of trees
swaying in winds not always off the sea,
but reaching out from far-off northern hills.

Ruth Bidgood

MIDDLETON HALL

Thistledown

Middleton Hall

An informal garden: walls of rose brick
flushed stone, lemony lichen, moulded
snail shells, stonecrop starred mauve
in the cracks, moss stubble, a barn
roofed with sloping air, damp rubble, broad
arches still sound, and the levelled ground
within the walls a plot of wilderness

where the sun grows unchecked, where
silence shuts out the world
like a cloche; where maincrop thistles
ripen and head, where nettles mulch themselves
in lazy beds, where gardener sheep move
methodically, clipping and trimming
these acres white with seeds

fleecy and pearled. Each corner's curved:
the boundaries breaking and blurred
a free for all. At the entrance gate
ivy twists ropes, clenched in the hinge-slot;
nails its macrame to the stone and knits
over brickwork. A staggered row
of plum trees clings to order, crabbed survivors

on parade, their branches furred with grey
unpruned, rotten, barren for years, lined up
for some forgotten purpose, skirted with nettles
waist-deep, dark, lush on a loam of plums.
Three buzzards float and wheel
over the old ice-house sunk in the hill -
their mewing pierces the stillness, rises, dies.

A wealthy cultivated past lies
under these ruins, latent as a pod
its blueprint stored in spore and leafmould:
twenty million pounds for a future dream
of splendour, bounty, a Disneyland of flowers
with trees, ponds, borders....only the present
stirs and shuffles. Sheep and thistledown

Hilary Llewellyn-Williams

Green Gift

Belle Vue Park, Newport

Belle Vue
across docks' blackened tide
but here green envelops
promenade terrace reflects
pagoda bandstand roof
while Lord Tredegar's landgift
pleases weekend strollers

Belle Vue
over glasshouses past
bowling green tennis courts
where skipping with two sisters
I climbed on twisted swings
seesaws and glittering slide
high above Cardiff road

wide view
neatly dressed we shuffled
carefully swept gravel
defied elusive keepers
butterflies tantalised
as we jumped to imprison
fragile vibrating wings

long view
of childhood excitement
in fluttering pleasures
those daring summer swingflights
in light skirts then scrambling
through spider-webbed shrubbery
spying on bowlers' games

BELLE VUE PARK

Belle Vue
such vibrant energies
colour-clustered in rows
with guardian butterflies
clasping emblazoned gates
opened above the threshold
of Newport's Otherworld

Alison Bielski

NATIONAL MUSEUM OF WALES

The Steps

In front of the museum
too expensive now for Cardiffians
where John Tripp hid
his bicycle clips among the pillars
and the statue of Lloyd George
greens slowly in the drizzle
I saw Tom Jones once
eluding fans among the bushes.

Heart of the Welsh universe
its white portland replicated
perfectly in India
where the architect made a quick
rupee reselling his plans.

The past concentrates on these slabs.
Memory of marches, meetings, passions,
hired coaches like cream river-boats
the steps cut like a ghat on the Ganges.
When the sea rises
the tide will reach here with ease.

Peter Finch

GARTHEWIN

Garthewin

It was such a long time ago,
And the memory plays false. Was
There a gatehouse and a gravelled
Drive, prospecting in a gold-rush of
Dense daffodils for the white
And many-windowed mansion, like
A proposition of Euclid
Laid out on the hillside's lectern?
The dragon rampant on the roof
Is certain, and a chapel too -
Some sacred fragment lodged within,
Far from Assisi.
       What I remember
Most about that house above the Elwy,
Valley of hospitality, is
The drawing-room, the purple sash
Of a monsignor, the warm court
Of guests, and towering over all -
Ednyfed Fychan in his blood,
A latter-day uchelwr
Robert Wynne, Garthewin, patriot,
Golden in the hearth-light of his hall,
And an opulence of daffodils.

Raymond Garlick

TRETOWER COURT

Tretower Court

The place is still haunted by three fair-haired children
with snakes coiled round their necks. Sheep are scattered like
daisies
near the bird-infested tower.
Light flows through what was the roof.

They go in and out
of the empty gallery rooms, always one door ahead of you.
Some day you'll surprise one who squints at the shining fields
and writes like Henry Vaughan.

Merryn Williams

BEAUPRE CASTLE

Meurig Dafydd To His Mistress

No word I huffed when Stradling urged the squire
to throw my eulogy on the fire.
The fiddlers laughed. I, snow-silent, proud,
did not melt. But I'm spitless now,
my pearl, my buttercup, my bread-fruit.
I rattle their silver in my pocket.
I have other stanzas for harp and lute,
other gullible lords to flatter.
What do I care for that big-bellied Englishman
that bugle, that small-beer, that puff-ball,
that dung-odoured sonneteer, John Stradling?

Does he sing perfect metre like Taliesin?
Not that gout-toed, goat-faced manikin.
What does he know of Welsh necks crayoned
by the axe, blood on our feet, our history?
Has he stood pensive at the tomb
of Morian, or Morial, or March?
Wept at any nervous harp, at the gloom
of a dirge for Llywelyn the Last,
or the lament by Lewis Glyn Cothi?
That fungoid, that bunt, that broken-wind,
that bog-bean, can't tell a song from a grunt.

Clean heart, my theology, my sweet-briar,
he'd put our heritage on the fire.
Each night he swigs mead in a safe bed -
never sleeps roofed only by the stars.
At noon, never signs the euphonious nine
sermons of the blackbird. O my lotus,
his lexicon is small compared to mine.
His verses are like standing urine - tepid.
My Welsh stanzas have more heat in them
than the tumbling flames in the fire-place
of the Minstrel Hall of Bewpyr.

Dannie Abse

HAFOD

Illumination

Thomas Johnes's great library at Hafod was destroyed by fire in 1807

Books were hurled five thousand feet
into the air; parchment and paper
roared up in the blast and wafted
miles away - a storm of blazing words.
Through flurries of charred print
illiterate men and women felt
the true heat of enlightenment -
like a reactor melting down. Picture
a woman as she kneels to wash thin rags,
and sees the water bearing something:
shoals of script; illuminated
fragments rippling past.
Is she aware of something lost;
some deprivation; an elusive brilliance?

Barry Simner

Notes on the Poems

'Beaupre Castle'
p. 21

The poem refers to the words inscribed on three small panels in Richard Bassett's storeyed porch, which read: 'Say cowdst thou ever fynd or ever heare or see worlldry wretche or coworrd prove a faithfull frynde to bee Richarde Bassett having to Wyf Katherine daughter of Sir Thomas John Knight Bwylt this porche with the Tonnes in Ano 1600, his yeres 65, his wyf 55'.

'The Abergavenny Murders' p. 25

In 1175 the owner of Abergavenny Castle, the notorious William de Braose, invited local Welsh leaders to a feast and then murdered them. The Welsh later sacked the castle in retaliation, killing many of its inhabitants.

'Cwm Merddog'
p. 33

The image of the infant boy derives from the practice in ancient classical and celtic mythology of sacrificing an infant to the gods as a blessing on the house. The Cucullati equate to the three Fates in Celto- Roman iconography.

'Portmeirion, An Advert' p. 49

Sir Clough Williams-Ellis, creator of Portmeirion, eccentric, often wore plus-fours with yellow socks.

'Adelina' p. 77

From 1878 to 1919 the famous opera singer Adelina Patti lived at Craig-y-nos Castle and much extended the gardens there.

'This Hand: Gregynog' p. 81

The sculpture of a hand at the beginning of the woodland walk at Gregynog was designed by Francis Hewlett.

'Catherine at Stouthall' p. 87

In January 1770 William Powell of Glanareth, below the Black Mountain of Carmarthenshire, was murdered by a gang which included his wife's lover, Billy Williams.

'Meurig Dafydd To His Mistress' p. 101

In 1603 a party took place at Beaupre, at which a local bard, Meurig Dafydd, read a praise-poem to the squire William Bassett. Afterwards Meurig Dafydd was asked if he had retained a copy. On learning that he had not, Bassett, urged on by the poet John Stradling, burned the praise-poem, saying:
"I swere yf there bee no copie of this extante, none shall there ever bee, and therewith put it sure enough into the fier."

Alphabetical Index to Sites

Note: Ownership and access added where applicable. In the case of privately
owned sites, permission must be granted by the owners before access
can be allowed.

Abergavenny Castle Abergavenny, Gwent
OS MAP 161 : NGR SO 299139
Local authority ownership
The original castle was a motte of earth and timber thrown up by Hamelin
de Balun before 1090, but by 1175 it had been replaced by a stone keep. Its
most substantial stonework is from the C13th and C14th. The seat of the
notorious William de Braose, it later passed to the Hastings family, and the
Nevilles. In the early C19th William Neville laid it out as a 'place of
recreation'. Burnt, attacked, and dismantled by Charles I, only fragments of
the castle survive. Part of the substantial curtain wall was landscaped into a
rockery, and a museum built over the original motte. Part of the walls and
gatehouse remain. It has been said that Abergavenny 'has been oftner stain'd
with the infamy of treachery, than any other castle in Wales' (William
Camden).

Aberglasney Llandeilo, Dyfed
OS MAP 159: NGR SN 579222
Private ownership: strictly no public access
Aberglasney was built around 1600 by Bishop Rudd, who built on top of an
older site. The Dyers enlarged it in the C18th, and it was the home of the
poet John Dyer. In the grounds are a yew tunnel, folly, and a unique parapet
walk. Other surviving features include a pond, arches and cryptoporticus
walls. It should be noted that the house and grounds are in a great state of
disrepair, and dangerous.

Beaupre (Bewpyr) Castle St. Hilary, Cowbridge, S. Glamorgan
OS MAP 170: NGR ST 009720
CADW
Beaupre is a medieval manor house, dating from the C14th, occupied by the
Bassett family, and constructed around two courtyards. In the C16th an

extensive rebuilding programme was started by Sir Rice Mansell, and
continued by William and Richard Bassett. In 1586 Richard Bassett built the
outer gatehouse, and in 1600 constructed Beaupre's focal point, the yellow
ashlar three-storeyed inner porch. It includes Doric, Ionic and Corinthian
columns, and the Bassett shield bearing their motto 'Gwell Angau Na
Chywilydd' (Better Death Than Dishonour). Beaupre, whose name derives
from the French 'beau-repaire', was the focus of a number of tales created by
Iolo Morganwg.

Belle Vue Park Casnewydd (Newport), Gwent
OS MAP 171: NGR ST 307872
Newport Borough Council
The park was opened in 1894 after Lord Tredegar gave c. 23 acres of land to
the town 'for the enjoyment of the people'. Designed by Thomas Mawson,
the sloping ground was landscaped with winding paths, trees and a rocky
stream. The town put in the gates, which bear the Newport arms and the
motto 'Terra Marique'. In 1910 terraces, a tea pavilion, Bandstand and a
unique pair of conservatories were added. The Council has now restored the
Bandstand, and the conservatories are listed for conservation. The park,
bordering the A48 Newport Road, also featured bowls, tennis, swings, see-
saw and slide. It retains the Gorsedd circle of stones from 1897, when
Newport hosted the National Eisteddfod.

Bertholey House Llantrisant, Gwent
OS MAP 171: NGR ST 397945
Private Ownership. No Public Access
An elegant mansion, built 1830 on an existing site above the Usk, and
enclosed within delicate garden railings. The original building included a
pilastered front, semicircular portico, and a glass-domed circular staircase
hall. In the drawing-room was a Sienna marble fireplace decorated with
doves and wreathes. On 15th March 1905 the owner, Philip Morel of Cardiff,
accidentally set fire to the building, and Bertholey has been a ruin since that
date, though the farm at the back is occupied and privately owned.

Bodfuan (Bodvean/Bodfean), Nr. Pwllheli, Llŷn, Gwynedd
OS MAP 123: NGR SH 326381
Private Ownership. No Public Access
Bodfuan Hall was the home of the Wynns, and dates from before 1500. In the

C16th John Wynn was standard-bearer to Edward VI, for which service he was also granted Cwrt Farm, Aberdaron, Bardsey Island and land in Caernarfonshire. Anne Boleyn frequently stayed at Bodfuan, and on her marriage to Henry VIII was given a considerable amount of land adjoining the estate, which she later bequeathed to the Wynns. The building is plain, but with richly wooded grounds, including huge beeches and rhododendrons. The nearby Romanesque church, designed by H. Kennedy, contains elegant monuments to members of the Wynn family.

Castell Coch   Nr. Tongwynlais, S. Glamorgan
OS MAP 171: NGR ST 131826
CADW
Named 'Red Castle' from the colour of its stone, Castell Coch was designed by William Burges for the Third Marquis of Bute, and inspired by the work of the French architect Viollet-Le-Duc. Begun in 1875, and erected on the site of a small C13th castle, the result was a 'sham' medieval castle, with conical tiled roofs and a working drawbridge and portcullis. Inside, Burges richly decorated the rooms in a mixture of styles, depicting mythological figures, animals, flowers and birds. The Lady's Bedroom is the most spectacular, with a domed and mirrored ceiling, the winged figure of Psyche, and an elaborate scarlet and gold bed with crystal globe bed-knobs.

Castell Henllys Iron Age Fort,   Nr. Eglwyswrw, Newport, Dyfed
OS MAP 145: NGR SN 117390
Pembrokeshire Coast National Park Authority, Dyfed County Council
The Castell Henllys site was purchased by the National Park Authority in 1991. Originally inhabited in the Romano-Celtic period, it is currently being reconstructed as an historical and interpretational facility. In an unusual experiment, roundhouses have been constructed using the original post-holes, and a range of ancient skills practised, based on techniques thought to have been used in the Iron Age. With visitor participation encouraged, the site is still being excavated, with plans for further reconstructions.

Craig-y-Nos Castle   Glyntawe, Powys
OS MAP 160: NGR SN 840153
House privately owned: grounds owned by National Trust
Craig-y-Nos, 'The Rock of Night', was designed by T.H. Wyatt and built in

1842 for Rhys Davies Powell. In 1886 it was bought by Adelina Patti. She made extensive improvements, including a clock tower, rockery, rose garden, lakes, and a Winter Garden. The latter is now the Patti Pavilion in Swansea. A theatre was built in 1891 inside the building, and regularly used for concerts. After Patti's death in 1919, the house became a hospital, before falling into disrepair. Sold in February 1995 into private ownership, plans are currently underway to restore the building.

Cwm Merddog Cwm, Ebbw Vale, Gwent
OS MAP 171: NGR SO 194044
Originally known as 'Cwm Merddog', Cwm lies south of Ebbw Vale and was an old farming settlement at the confluence of the Merddog brook and the Ebbw Fawr. The present village was built to serve the Marine Colliery sunk there in the middle of the C19th during the industrial development of Ebbw Vale, when the name was changed to 'Cwm'. The buildings of the old Marine Colliery were demolished to provide the car-park for Garden Festival Wales in 1992. The Miners' Institute collapsed a few years ago due to subsidence from the colliery. The slag heaps from the steelworks became the site of the Garden Festival itself, a central feature of which was the elegant Japanese waterfall.

Dinefwr Llandeilo, Dyfed
OS MAP 159: NGR SN 612217
Dyfed Wildlife Trust/National Trust
Seat of the great Lord Rhys ap Gruffydd, Dinefwr dates back to the C9th and was associated with Hywel Dda and the kingdom of Deheubarth. The remains of the castle, currently undergoing restoration work by CADW, date from the C12th and include a large keep-tower, to which a gazebo was added in the C17th. By 1523 the castle was abandoned when descendants of the Lord Rhys built Newton House, which was refurbished in both the C17th and the 1860's. Much park landscaping was carried out by George Rice in the 1770's. Dinefwr also has a C16th deer-park, with over 100 fallow deer, and the famous White Park Cattle, established in the C10th. The herd, dispersed in 1976, has now been re-established.

Garden Festival Site, Vale of Ebbw, Gwent
OS MAP 171: NGR SO 168078
Blaenau Gwent Borough Council/Gwent County Council
Garden Festival Wales was held from 1st May-4th October 1992 at Blaenau, on the abandoned site of the Ebbw Vale Steelworks. Between 1760 and 1850 iron works, coal mines and railways shaped the industrial landscape of the area, and it suffered from the subsequent running down of these industries. It was hoped the Festival would help regenerate the local economy. Work began in 1986 on reclaiming 142 acres of derelict land, and planting over 1½ million trees, shrubs, plants and bulbs. Attractions included the Garden of Welsh Myth and Magic, fun rides, flower pavilions, water features and on-site live events. Following the Festival, plans were made to build a village on the site, thus establishing a new community in the area.

Garthewin Llanfair Talhaiarn, Clwyd
OS MAP 116: NGR SH 914704
Privately owned. No public access
Garthewin has been in continuous habitation by the Wynne family, whose connection with the area goes back to the C9th, and who trace their descent through Ednyfed Fychan, Seneschal of Gwynedd from 1215, and chief counsellor to Llywelyn the Great. The present mansion was built c. 1710 and enlarged by Robert Wynne 1767-1772. Later additions include a drawing-room, gatehouse, loggia and Catholic chapel. Clough Williams-Ellis restored Garthewin in 1930. In recent years it has become celebrated for its Welsh theatre, in a barn converted by T.S. Tait. One of the original brick arches became the proscenium, and the first performance of a number of Saunders Lewis's plays were given there.

Gelli Aur Llandeilo, Dyfed
OS MAP 159: NGR SN 595198
Dyfed County Council
Once the seat of the Earls of Cawdor, the original building lay in a large landscape park in the Tywi valley. Owned by the Vaughan family, the valley was celebrated by John Dyer in his poem 'Grongar Hill'. In the C18th, extensive tree-planting was carried out, specimens including Spanish chestnut, beech, spruce, fir and Weymouth pine. The present house is Tudor in style, with stepped gables and a gabled tower, and was designed by Sir Jeffrey Wyatville after the original building had been demolished. Dating from 1832, it now houses the County Agricultural College.

Gregynog Tregynon,.Powys
OS MAP 136: NGR SO 085975
University of Wales
A black-and-white C19th house, rebuilt on an earlier structure. Owned
successively by the Blayney family and the Barons Sudeley and Joicey, until
taken over in 1920 by Gwendoline and Margaret Davies. The Davies sisters
planted on a large scale, and created a pool garden, duck pond, woodlands
and a dell. Under them Gregynog also flourished as a centre for the arts, and
was renowned for its festivals, as well as its library, paintings, and famous
Press. After the death of Gwendoline, Margaret Davies gave Gregynog to the
University of Wales in 1962 to be used as a venue 'for the cultivation and
enjoyment of the arts.'

Gwrych Castle Abergele, Clwyd
OS MAP 116: NGR SH 928775
Privately owned: no public access
A C19th castellated mansion created by Lloyd Bamford Hesketh together
with G.A. Busby, between 1822 and 1853. The structure included a series of
long battlements strung out along the hillside, with numerous circular and
rectangular towers and turrets. The park and garden were similarly
crenellated. Most of the windows are iron, cast at the Mersey Foundry owned
by John Cragg. A list of genuine and legendary historical events connected
with the locality is inscribed at the entrance. The castle is now in a state of
disrepair.

Hafod Cwm Ystwyth, Dyfed
OS MAP 135: NGR SN 760731
Forestry Enterprise
Hafod is most famous for the work of Thomas Johnes, who inherited the
estate in 1780. In 1786 he built a Gothic mansion, designed by Thomas
Baldwin and extended by John Nash. Johnes landscaped the grounds in the
Picturesque manner, planting several million trees, and creating two circuit
walks. Features included bridges, waterfalls, the Robber's Cave, an obelisk
and ice-house, Mrs. Johnes's Flower Garden and Mariamne's Garden.
Coleridge visited the area, and Hafod was possibly the inspiration for ' Kubla
Khan'. In 1807 fire destroyed the interior of the house, including the art
collection and octagonal domed library. Though rebuilt, financial ruin and

the death of Marianne caused Johnes to leave Hafod. He died in 1816. The house was later improved, and an Italianate campanile and terrace added in 1853, but it became derelict and was blown up as unsafe in 1958. The Welsh Historic Gardens Trust currently have a restoration project ongoing at Hafod.

Kidwelly Castle   Kidwelly, Dyfed
OS MAP 159: NGR SN 409071
CADW
A well-preserved C12th concentric castle overlooking the River Gwendraeth, and established by Bishop Roger of Salisbury c.1106. In Norman control for many years, and frequently attacked by Welsh forces, it was extensively rebuilt and modified over the centuries by successive owners. The castle consists of a C14th semicircular outer ward, and a C13th inner ward with four corner turrets, a twin-towered gatehouse and a curtain wall. The gatehouse is the most impressive feature, containing three arches, drawbridge, portcullis and 'murder holes'. The castle was abandoned in the C16th.

Llandaff Court (now Insole Court) Llandaff, S. Glamorgan
OS MAP 171: NGR ST 150779
City of Cardiff
Originally known as Ely Court, the small house, grounds and pond were bought in the C19th by James Insole the coal shipper. By 1873 an elaborate Victorian house with bays and gables was completed for him by E.J. Robinson. A large carriage porch was later added. The house includes a decorated chapel, with carvings both inside and on the ornamental balustrading in the grounds. The 9 acres of garden were planted with specimen trees, alpines, rare plants and the iris beds created by Violet Insole. The grounds also included a walled peach shelter, courtyard, tunnels, yew hedges and paths. Cardiff Corporation purchased the property from Eric Insole in 1932. It is currently owned and maintained by Cardiff City Council.

Llanerchaeron   Aberaeron, Dyfed
OS MAP 146: NGR SN 479602
National Trust
In Tudor times, the estate belonged to the Parry family, but passed to the Lewises in the C17th, who occupied it for some 200 years. The present

house, surviving virtually intact, was designed by John Nash in 1794-5 for
Colonel William Lewis, cousin to Thomas Johnes. The layout is planned in
the Picturesque style, with house, farm buildings, church and cottages
integrated into the landscape. The farm buildings are arranged in a series of
courtyards. A billiard room, water wheel and bailiff's house were later added.
The grounds include two walled gardens, one housing the Welsh Daffodil
Collection, an ornamental lake, and extensive parkland. The last owner, John
Powell Ponsonby Lewes, bequeathed Llanerchaeron to the National Trust on
his death in 1989.

Llanmihangel Place Llanmihangel, S. Glamorgan
OS MAP 170: NGR SS 981719
Private ownership. No public access
An attractive mid-late C16th towered house, partly castellated, now in use as
a farm. For generations the seat of the Thomas family, and sold to Sir
Humphrey Edwin in the C17th. Edwin laid out half-formal terraced gardens,
including an orchard, hollies, cypresses, a windbreak of sycamores, and the
avenue of huge yews that was its main feature. The saddleback tower of
Llanmihangel Church juts out of a wooded dell, beside a pool where the
C15th heiress Eleanor Dee was drowned. Branded as a witch, it is said that
her ghost can still be seen rising in the white mists that gather at twilight.

Llantarnam Abbey Llantarnam, Cwmbrân, Gwent
OS MAP 171: NGR ST 312930
Private ownership. No public access
The Cistercian Abbey was founded here from Strata Florida in 1171, at the
invitation of Hywel ap Iorwerth, Lord of Caerleon. In 1835-7 T.H. Wyatt
rebuilt it as an Elizabethan Gothic house for Reginald Blewitt, incorporating
fragments from the Abbey. The garden terrace is surrounded by a castellated
wall with corner bastions, and the park and forecourt are entered under
Tudor archways. A large kneeling figure of a monk remains from the grotto;
surviving stone statues include a musketeer, archer and pilgrim. The nearby
C13th tithe barn survives.

Maen Twrog Maentwrog, Merioneth, Gwynedd
OS MAP 124: NGR SH 664406
A single standing-stone set against the west wall of Maentwrog church-yard -
an erratic, and described as a 'glacier-rolled granitic boulder'. According to

legend, it was hurled from the top of Moelwyn Bach by the Celtic saint St. Twrog (son of Ithel Hael) onto a pagan altar. The imprint of St. Twrog's fingers and thumb are said to be still visible on the stone. St. Twrog died in AD 610 and the original church may have dated from this time. Maen Tyriawg is also mentioned in the Mabinogion as the burial-place of Pryderi.

Margam Country Park   Port Talbot, West Glamorgan
OS MAP 170: NGR SN 803862
West Glamorgan County Council
Now a Country Park, among its attractions Margam retains its famous Orangery, Castle and Abbey ruins. The C12th Cistercian Abbey was dissolved in 1537, and Sir Thomas Rice Mansel acquired the estate between 1540 and 1557. By the late C17th, Margam had a large banqueting house and landscaped grounds. In 1787 the Orangery was built by Anthony Keck to protect Mansel's rare collection of citrus trees. Changes in the C19th included the building of Margam Castle, designed by Thomas Hopper for Christopher Rice Mansel Talbot, and the demolition of the old village to create a kitchen garden. The estate was bought by the Council in 1974 and the Country Park created, with ongoing restoration work to the ruins.

Middleton Hall   Llanarthne, Dyfed
OS MAP 159: NGR SN 521182
Dyfed County Council/National Trust (Paxton's Tower)
A neo-classical house built 1793-5, and created for Sir William Paxton by S.P. Cockerell, who also designed Paxton's Tower. The park was landscaped with lakes, cascades, rock-pools, bridges and mineral springs. The house was demolished in 1931 after a fire, but the end wing and stables remain. Various features of the park survive, including an egg-shaped ice-house, an unusual double-walled kitchen garden, and a curving annexe thought to have been used for herbs. Part of the grounds are currently undergoing extensive restoration under the Council's Manpower Scheme.

National Museum of Wales, Cathays Park, Cardiff
OS Map 171: NGR ST 185769
City of Cardiff
In 1898 the land which became known as Cathays Park was sold to the City of Cardiff by Lord Bute, and from 1904 onwards the Edwardian Civic Centre

of bright Portland stone was built. The National Museum was designed in 1920 by A. Dunbar Smith and Cecil Brewer, and formally opened by King George V in 1927. The building has since been enlarged. Built in neo-classical style, the frontage has a recessed Doric portico, angle pavilions, and a large dome above the wide flight of entrance steps.

Pentre Ifan Burial Chamber Nr. Newport, Dyfed
OS MAP 145: NGR SN 099370
CADW
Commanding a wide view over the Nevern valley, Pentre Ifan lies on the northern foothills of the Preselis. One of the finest Neolithic cromlechs in Britain, the chamber is a portal dolmen, with a 16½ft long capstone, supported by three uprights. It is believed to have originally lain at the end of a cairn roughly 120 ft long. Built from stone from the Preseli hills, which also provided the famous circle of 'blue stones' at Stonehenge, the chamber is approximately 4-5000 years old.

Plas yn Rhiw Nr. Aberdaron, Gwynedd: Llŷn Peninsula
OS MAP 123: NGR SH 237282
National Trust
A small C17th manor house, originally medieval, overlooking Porth Neigwl (Hell's Mouth). Enlarged in the early C18th and modernised in the Regency period, when a shallow-pitched roof and verandah were added. From 1939 onwards the three Misses Keating lived there. They restored and planted the garden, which now includes woodlands, rhododendrons, magnolias, azaleas, sub-tropical shrubs and ornamental gardens.

Portmeirion Penrhyndeudraeth, Gwynedd
OS MAP 124: NGR SH 589370
Portmeirion Trust
Inspired by Italian coastal villages such as Portofino, Portmeirion was created by Sir Clough Williams-Ellis. After purchasing the old mansion of Aber Iâ, he added Castell Deudraeth to the property. In 1926 work began on a cluster of Italianate pastel-coloured buildings placed round a central courtyard flanked by a campanile and dome. The C19th mansion was converted into an elaborate hotel, and a mixture of architectural styles and features used, many

originating from other structures: Williams-Ellis was to call Portmeirion a 'Home for Fallen Buildings'. He also created the Gwyllt, where a dense growth of exotic plants complement the eclectic range of architecture. Portmeirion has been used as a film set on many occasions, most notably for the television series 'The Prisoner'.

Powis Castle   Welshpool, Powys
OS MAP 126: NGR SJ 218063
National Trust
Adapted from a medieval fortress founded by Owain ap Gruffydd. The castle is of red sandstone, and was bought by the Herbert family in 1587. The formal gardens, perhaps the finest hanging gardens in Britain, were laid out in the Restoration period and later revitalised by the fourth Earl of Powys. They include a series of dramatic C17th terraces, arches, clipped yews, urns, figures and an Orangery. In the valley below, formal water gardens are ornamented with trees and shrubs.

St. Trillo's Chapel Rhos-on-Sea, Clwyd
OS MAP 116: NGR SH 842812
Church in Wales
A small building of boulders, 11ft x 8 ft, standing on the sea-shore within reach of the highest spring tides, and sheltering a small spring which traditionally represents the well of the patron saint of the parish. The building is plain-roofed and roughly vaulted, and thought to have been built by the monks of Aberconwy Abbey in the C16th (other sources date it from C6th-C16th). The roof collapsed in the 1850's, but was restored, and the chapel re-consecrated by Bishop Havard on St. Trillo's Day (16th June) 1935.

Stouthall Reynoldston, S. Glamorgan
OS MAP 159: NGR SS 475893
Private ownership. No public access
The Lucas family have lived in the Gower peninsula for over 500 years, and the Reynoldston branch was well-established by the reign of Elizabeth I. The old house at Stouthall was a 7-hearth farmhouse. Rebuilt for John and Catherine Lucas c. 1793, it was designed by William Jernegan, who had settled in Swansea in the 1780's. A severe, three-storey villa in Palladian style,

it has symmetrical facades and Adam-inspired interior decoration. The garden facade is reminiscent of nearby Penrice Castle. John Lucas also laid out a park of approximately 40 acres, complete with stables, grotto, ice house and imitation stone circle. Note: the house was repainted in 1992 and is no longer yellow.

Tan-yr-Allt Tremadoc, Gwynedd
OS MAP 124: NGR SH 568405
Steiner Organisation: private ownership
A long, white verandahed Regency house, built in 1800 by William Madocks. Madocks purchased the estate in 1798, and recovered c. 2000 acres of Penmorva Marsh. An act of Parliament enabled him to reclaim the Traeth Mawr from Pont Aberglaslyn to Gest, where he created Tremadoc. Situated above the town, Tan-yr-Allt has the low-pitched roof and deep eaves characteristic of Madocks' style, and enabled by the high quality of the area's slate. From 1812-13 Shelley rented Tan-yr-Allt—where part of Queen Mab was written—but quarrelled with neighbours after allegedly agitating among local workers. The Shelleys left after the house was broken into and warning shots fired. The dense oak forest around the house is now a nature conservation area.

Tretower Court Tretower Village, Nr. Crickhowell, Powys
OS MAP 161: NGR SO 186211
CADW
A well-preserved C14th manor house, built around a grassy courtyard, Tretower derives its name from the large stone C13th keep belonging to the medieval motte-and-bailey castle nearby. Between the C15th-C18th it was the seat of the Vaughan family, and home of the metaphysical poet Henry Vaughan. The family crest—three children with snakes around their necks—is still visible. In the C15th Sir Roger Vaughan completely reconstructed Tretower, adding an extensive west range and a wooden gallery. Later additions include a wall-walk and a gate-house.

Bibliography and Site Acknowledgement

I am indebted to the following poets, for help with the site-notes:
Raymond Garlick
Alison Bielski
Sheenagh Pugh
Ruth Bidgood

Acknowledgement is also due to Elisabeth Whittle, the CADW series of publications, Sian Spink of the National Monuments Record, and to the publications listed below, which are also included as further reading material:

D Renn, *Norman Castles in Britain* (London, 1973)
E. Whittle, *Glamorgan and Gwent* (HMSO, 1992)
C. Barber and J.G. Williams, *The Ancient Stones of Wales* (Blorenge, 1989)
J. Tillotson, *Picturesque Scenery in Wales* (T.J. Allman, 1861)
D. Robinson, *Heritage in Wales* (CADW, 1989)
CADW, *Wales: Castles and Historic Places* (CADW, 1990)
W. Vaughan-Thomas and A. Llewellyn, *The Shell Guide to Wales* (Michael Joseph, 1969)
B. Bell, *Insight Guides: Wales* (APA Publications, 1989)
J. Hilling, *Cardiff and the Valleys* (Lund Humphries, 1973)
P. Smith, *Houses of the Welsh Countryside* (HMSO, 1975)
J. Hilling, *The Historical Architecture of Wales* (University of Wales Press, 1976)
R. Hammond, *Complete Wales* (Ward Lock and Co., 1966)
E. Hubbard, *The Buildings of Wales* (University of Wales Press, 1986)
E. Beazley and P. Howell, *The Companion Guide to North Wales* (Collins, 1975)
E. Beazley and P. Howell, *The Companion Guide to South Wales* (Collins, 1977)
G.T. Hughes, P. Morgan, J.G. Thomas, *Gregynog* (University of Wales Press, 1977)
E. Whittle, *The Historic Gardens of Wales* (CADW, 1992)
Robert Lucas, *A Gower Family* (1986)
Thomas Lloyd, *The Lost Houses of Wales* (SAVE Britain's Heritage, 1986)